Heavenly Hugs

by
Hannah Grace

First published by AuthorHouse 01/16/2006

ISBN: 1-4208-7491-8 (sc)

Library of Congress Control Number: 2005909882

Printed in the United States of America
Bloomington, Indiana

This book is printed on acid-free paper.

authorHOUSE

1663 LIBERTY DRIVE
BLOOMINGTON, INDIANA 47403
(800) 839-8640
www.authorhouse.com

Acknowledgements:

I want to first acknowledge God for giving me the ability to write and to express His love and compassion. I also want to acknowledge my church home family for their love and support especially as I have taken on this project; your prayers and friendship have added sunshine to my days! I also want to acknowledge and thank all the hard working Doctors, nurses and other health care professionals who spend their life helping those who are ill. May your lives be blessed for all your hard work and choosing to help the helpless and trying to ease their pain and find new cures for diseases. May God reward you for all that you do; thank you.

Dedication:

I lovingly dedicate this book to Mr. & Mrs. Reid Estes and to Mr. & Mrs. Dale Linder. The influence that you have had on my life through your faithfulness to God, and by your acts of kindness, compassion and love towards me are firmly embedded in my heart. All the days of my life have been blessed by the gifts of your friendship and for that, I am forever grateful.
With much love always-Hannah Grace

I am just a small child in a sad world of hurts.

I don't always know why I hurt but my angel is with me.

When the nighttime comes along and the darkness steals my song;

Angel wings surround me with heavenly hugs to hold me.

My tired eyes close now for sweet dreams to be mine;

For I know my Father in Heaven is always watching in love.

When there are tender tears of sadness and pain is all over my body,

Angels surround my presence embracing my fears with much gentle care.

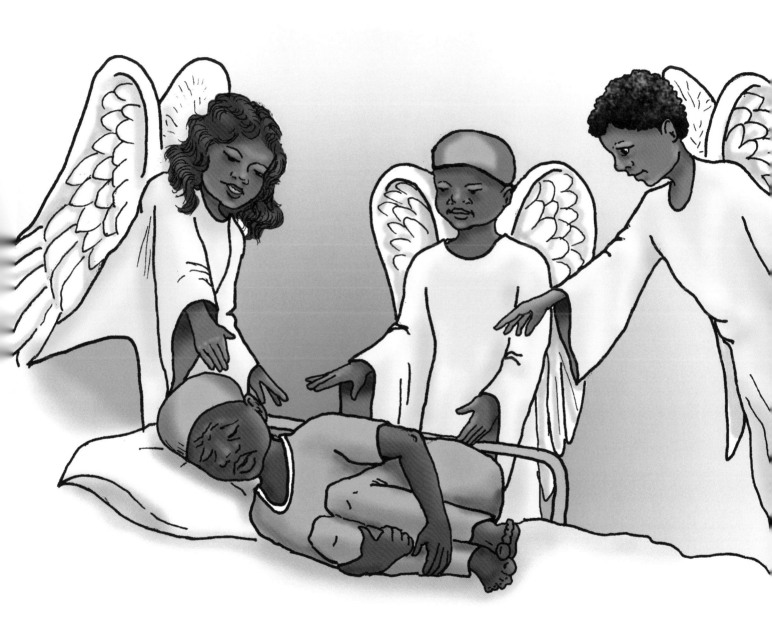

Jesus loves me because He does provide an angel to sing me lullabies.

When I awake in the morning light sometimes I feel good and some times I feel bad.

Yet no matter how I feel I know that angels are watching over me.

Whispering songs that make me giggle and laugh or they sing to me sweet nursery rhymes.

I don't know what my day may bring and there are times I just want to scream.

I hurt so bad and my body aches with pain. I want to go out and play.

Dear God in Heaven please send to me an angel to listen to my every need.

My special friend sent from above to be with me no matter what.

Jesus loves me this I know for my angel is with me and tells me so.

My tired eyes now close for the night with lullabies of love from my angel friend.

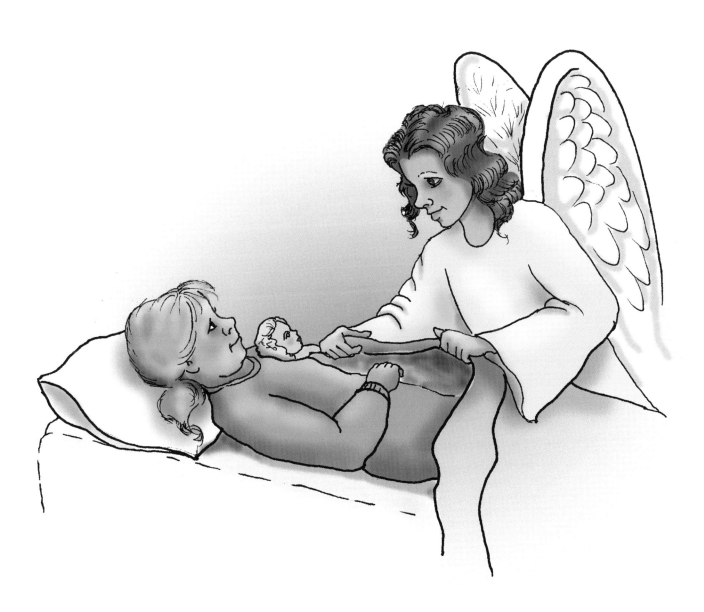

God loves His precious children so He sends from above Heavenly hugs to watch over me with much love.

Psalm 91:11 For He will give His angels charge over you to keep you in all your ways.

Dear God:

_____

_____

_____

_____

_____

_____

_____

_____

_____

_____

_____

_____

_____

_____

Dear God:

_____

_____

_____

_____

_____

_____

_____

_____

_____

_____

_____

_____

_____

_____

Dear God:

_____

_____

_____

_____

_____

_____

_____

_____

_____

_____

_____

_____

_____

The author, Hannah Grace, resides near the nation's capitol.

I enjoy writing and have been writing since the age of eight. My dream in life was to become a published author and that is now taking place. I also enjoy time with family and friends. Life is short-we must embrace all of it! I want for people to feel loved and to know that they are loved unconditionally. My prayer is that the life that God has given me will be lived in such a way that the words I write and the stories you read will let you see and know my Father in Heaven...regardless of your life situation there is a God-a benevolent God who loves you with an everlasting love and wants you to know Him.

Dear Friend,
I want you to know that you are special to my Father in Heaven. He loves you and it is my heart's desire that through these words; you will embrace our Father's love.
With love,
Hannah Grace

Printed in the United States
149460LV00002B